GETTING TO KNOW THE WORLD'S GREATEST
INVENTORS & SCIENTISTS

CHARLES
DREW

Doctor Who Got the World Pumped Up to Donate Blood

WRITTEN AND ILLUSTRATED BY MIKE VENEZIA

CHILDREN'S PRESS®
AN IMPRINT OF SCHOLASTIC INC.
NEW YORK TORONTO LONDON AUCKLAND SYDNEY
MEXICO CITY NEW DELHI HONG KONG
DANBURY, CONNECTICUT

Reading Consultant: Nanci R. Vargus, Ed.D., Assistant Professor, School of Education, University of Indianapolis

Photographs © 2009: akg-Images, London: 24; Alamy Images/Phototake Inc.: 20; Corbis Images: 7 (Bettmann), 21, 25, 26 (Hulton-Deutsch Collection), 17 (Rudy Sulgan), 29; Getty Images/Alfred Eisenstaedt/Time Life Pictures: 3; Moorland Spingarn Research Center, Howard University, Washington, D.C.: 10, 12, 14, 16, 23, 30, 31 (Prints and Photographs); The Image Works/Alinari Archives: 6.

Colorist for illustrations: Andrew Day

Library of Congress Cataloging-in-Publication Data

Venezia, Mike.
  Charles Drew : doctor who got the world pumped up to donate blood / written and illustrated by Mike Venezia.
      p. cm. — (Getting to know the world's greatest inventors and scientists)
  includes index.
  ISBN-13: 978-0-531-23725-0 (lib. bdg.) 978-0-531-21334-6 (pbk.)
  ISBN-10: 0-531-23725-7 (lib. bdg.)   0-531-21334-X (pbk.)
  1. Drew, Charles, 1904-1950—Juvenile literature. 2. African American surgeons—Biography—Juvenile literature. 3. Surgeons—United States—Biography—Juvenile literature. 4. Blood banks—United States—Juvenile literature. I. Title.
  RD27.35.D74V46 2009
  617.092—dc22
  [B]
                          2008027648

1 2 3 4 5 6 7 8 9 10 R 18 17 16 15 14 13 12 11 10 09

Dr. Charles Drew, shown here in 1946, was an authority on preparing and storing blood for blood transfusions.

Charles Richard Drew was born on June 3, 1904, in Washington, D.C. Charles Drew succeeded at everything he did. He was a great scientist, doctor, surgeon, teacher, and athlete. Dr. Drew's discoveries in the field of **blood transfusions** helped save the lives of thousands of people.

Dr. Charles Drew found ways for people to safely donate and receive blood. He also helped develop a system, called a **blood bank**, to store large amounts of blood for long periods of time. Blood banks made it possible for more people to get blood quickly if they needed it during surgery or after a serious injury.

Although Charles Drew developed more successful ways to store and use blood, he

didn't invent blood transfusions. Hundreds of years ago, doctors started trying to give people blood to replace blood lost after injuries. As long ago as 1667, a French doctor tried transferring lamb's blood into a patient, but it didn't work. Doctors didn't really understand what blood was made of or how to transfer it from person to person until the early 1900s, when Charles Drew was a kid.

Charles Drew was raised in the nation's capital, Washington, D.C.
This is how the city looked when Charles was a young boy.

As a kid, Charles was known as Charlie. Charlie
grew up in a loving family. The Drews lived in
an area of Washington, D.C., near the Potomac
River. Because it was so foggy there, Charlie's
neighborhood was called Foggy Bottom.

Charlie's family had just barely enough money
to keep from being poor. Charlie's father was a
carpet installer. His mother had a teaching degree,
but decided to stay at home full-time to raise
her family.

The Drews were African American. Charlie grew up during a time when there was a lot of **racial prejudice** in the United States. Much of the country, including Washington, D.C., was **segregated**. Black citizens were separated from white citizens. African Americans had to use separate restaurants, movie theaters, schools, bathrooms, and swimming pools. They also were kept out of many jobs and were denied many basic rights, such as voting.

A man drinks from a segregated water fountain in the early 1900s.

Mr. and Mrs. Drew taught their children not to let the prejudice of others stand in their way. They taught them to get a good education, work hard, and achieve whatever goals they set for themselves.

All the Drew children were expected to bring home top grades, attend church every Sunday, and help around the house with daily chores. To save money, they were taught how to sew and patch their own clothes. Sewing was a skill that came in handy for Charlie later on, when he became a surgeon.

Charles Drew (first row, third from left) was both an excellent student and a star athlete at Dunbar High School.

Washington, D.C., had segregated schools when Charlie was growing up. But some of its schools for African-American students were among the best schools in the United States. Charlie went to one of those schools—Dunbar High School. Dunbar hired excellent teachers and set very high standards for its students.

While Charlie was at Dunbar, it became clear that he wasn't just a great student, but also a great athlete. He became a star on Dunbar's swimming, football, basketball, track, and baseball teams. Between studying and practicing sports, it's amazing that Charlie could keep all his activities straight! Charles Drew did so well in sports that he won an **athletic scholarship** to attend Amherst College in Massachusetts.

Here Charlie (wearing tie) is shown with three of his siblings (clockwise from right): Elsie, Nora, and Joseph. Charlie and his family were devastated when Elsie died of tuberculosis at the age of twelve.

Charlie took him up on his offer. It was an important moment in helping Charlie decide his future. He was fascinated to see how doctors treated patients in emergency situations. After this experience, Charles Drew was sure he wanted to become a doctor.

In 1926, Charles Drew graduated from Amherst College. Not only had he brought fame to Amherst on the playing field, but he graduated with top grades. Charles Drew had everything going for him, except for one thing—money! Charles didn't have nearly enough money to pay for medical school. So right away, he took a job as a teacher and coach at Morgan College in Baltimore, Maryland.

After he graduated from Amherst, Drew worked as a chemistry and biology teacher at Morgan College. He also coached the school's sports teams. Here he is shown (back row, far right) with the college's basketball team.

Drew attended medical school at McGill University in Montreal, Canada (above).

Finally, after working for two years, he had saved up enough for medical school. Charles applied to and was accepted at McGill University's medical school in Montreal, Canada.

Even though Charles took his studies seriously, he still found time for sports. He even set records for McGill's track team. After five years, Charles graduated at the top of his class. In 1933, Charles Drew achieved his dream. He had become a doctor of medicine.

While in medical school, Charles had become interested in the science of blood. He learned that it was very difficult to donate and store blood safely. Everyone in the world has one of four major blood types: Type A, B, AB, or O. A person needing blood has to be matched up with the correct blood type, or they could die.

During Dr. Drew's time, the big problem was how to store all the different blood types long enough so there would be enough blood available for whoever needed it. Blood could be kept for only about seven days before it spoiled. Sometimes, when a hospital ran out of the correct blood type, they would have to try and find a donor to match the patient's blood type. By the time they found someone, it might be too late.

Dr. Drew wanted to find a solution to this problem. After medical school, he spent several years improving his skills as a doctor, surgeon, and teacher. Then he turned his attention to solving the problem of blood storage.

In 1938, Charles Drew was awarded a **fellowship** to do research on blood at Columbia University's medical school in New York City. While at Columbia, he made an important discovery about blood **plasma**.

Plasma is the clear liquid in which blood cells float. Dr. Drew discovered that it was **red blood cells**, the cells that carry oxygen throughout the body, that were causing the problem in storing blood. Red blood cells spoil after just a few days. Dr. Drew found that if you removed red blood cells, the remaining plasma could be preserved for weeks.

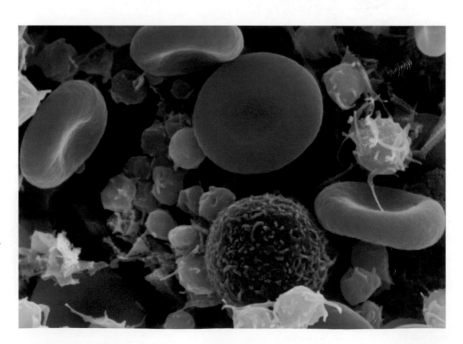

This is a magnified view of human blood cells. Dr. Drew discovered that blood could be stored longer if the red blood cells (shown in red) were removed from plasma.

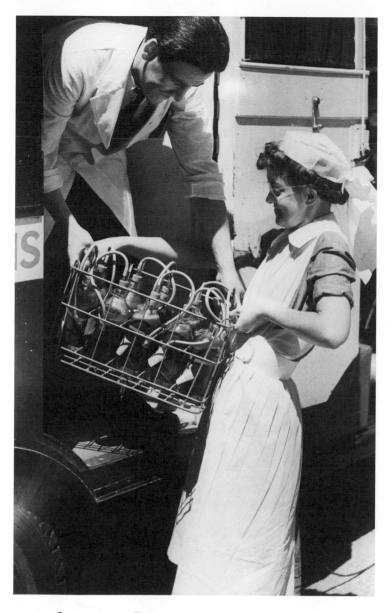

Dr. Drew developed better ways to process, store, and ship blood. This 1941 photograph shows a nurse transporting donated blood into a refrigerated van.

Another good thing about plasma is that it doesn't contain any red cells, so there's no need to worry about matching it to one of the four different blood types. Anybody could use any plasma. In an emergency situation, plasma could keep people alive until their bodies could make more blood on their own. While directing a blood bank at Columbia, Dr. Drew developed ways to freeze or dry plasma so that it could be shipped to wherever it was needed.

During this busy time, Dr. Drew managed to fall in love and get married. Charles met his future bride, Lenore Robbins, during a trip to a medical **conference**. Charles and Lenore were married in 1939. They eventually had four children. Charles Drew, who had always had a good sense of humor, nicknamed their first daughter "BeBe" after "blood bank."

Charles Drew with his wife, Lenore, and their four children

In 1940, Dr. Drew finished his studies at Columbia University. He then continued his research on blood at Howard University in Washington, D.C.

As it turned out, Dr. Drew's important discoveries about blood storage came just in the nick of time. World War II, which would become one of the most destructive, deadly wars in history, was just starting in Europe.

A London neighborhood after a German bomb attack in 1940

The German **dictator** Adolf Hitler and his armies were determined to take over Europe. London, England, was being bombed constantly by Germany. Injured soldiers and citizens there needed blood desperately. Dr. Drew was asked to return to New York to help run a program called "Blood for Britain." The British needed thousands of units of blood right away. Only a man like Dr. Charles Drew could have handled such a huge task.

Dr. Drew began by setting up blood banks to collect donations all over New York City. He then ordered trucks to be equipped with storage refrigerators and nurses to collect blood in areas outside the city. The plasma was removed, frozen or dried, and shipped overseas.

The Blood for Britain program was a huge success. Dr. Drew's discoveries helped save the lives of thousands of people in England.

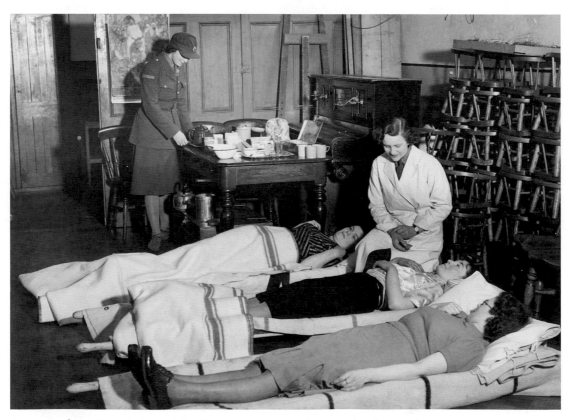

As part of Dr. Drew's Blood for Britain program, thousands of people donated blood to be shipped overseas.

An American soldier is given blood plasma behind enemy lines in 1944.

In 1941, the United States entered World War II. Now America needed its own emergency blood supply. Once again, Dr. Drew was called upon, this time to head up the Red Cross National Blood Collection program.

Unfortunately, while Dr. Drew was setting up the program, he suffered one of the greatest disappointments of his life. He learned that the U.S. military had decided not to accept blood donations from African Americans. Because of the army's prejudice, even Dr. Drew was unable to donate blood! Drew and other scientists knew that there was absolutely no difference between blood from white people and blood from African-American people. Dr. Drew was hurt, angry, and insulted. He had spent his life trying to overcome the fear and **ignorance** that caused prejudice.

Charles Drew protested the decision to exclude African-American blood. The military eventually agreed to accept the blood of African Americans but insisted that it be segregated from that of whites.

Dr. Drew was deeply disappointed. As soon as the national blood program was up and running smoothly, he resigned his post and returned to Howard University in Washington, D.C. There he began working on what he believed to be his greatest accomplishment.

Howard University is a historically black college. It was started right after the Civil War, in 1866, to educate former slaves. In the 1940s, Howard University's medical school didn't have a very strong reputation. Dr. Drew helped change that. He dedicated the rest of his life to teaching and training African-American medical students. Dr. Drew was a fantastic teacher who inspired many students.

Students in the bacteriology laboratory at Howard University in the early 1900s

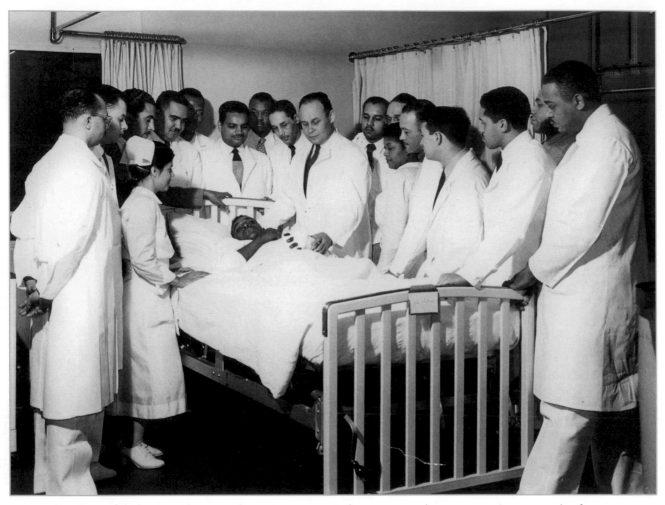

Dr. Drew felt that teaching and inspiring young doctors was the most important work of all. Here Dr. Drew (center) examines a patient as some of his medical students look on.

Charles Drew didn't want to turn out doctors who were just good—he wanted to turn out doctors and surgeons who were the best in the country. Dr. Charles Drew achieved his goal. Many of his graduates went on to become the very best surgeons in the United States.

Sadly, on April 1, 1950, Dr. Charles Drew died in a car accident while on his way to a medical conference. He was only forty-five years old.

Dr. Charles Drew was an outstanding doctor, scientist, and teacher. Although his life was cut short, his accomplishments saved many lives and have inspired thousands of people in the world of medicine.

Dr. Charles Drew gives a speech just a few days before his death.

Glossary

athletic scholarship (ath-LET-ik SKOL-ur-ship) An award of financial aid that a college offers to a student based on the student's superior athletic ability

blood bank (BLUHD BANGK) A place where blood is donated and stored; stored blood is used to replace blood lost by someone after an accident or during an operation

blood transfusion (BLUHD transs-FYOO-zhuhn) The injection of blood from one person into the body of another person who is injured or ill

conference (KON-fur-uhnss) A formal meeting for discussing ideas and opinions

dictator (DIK-tay-tur) Someone who has complete control of a country, often ruling it unjustly

fellowship (FEL-oh-ship) An agreement in which a university pays a student to conduct advanced study or research on a specific subject

ignorance (IG-nur-uhnss) Lack of knowledge and understanding

plasma (PLAZ-muh) The clear, yellow liquid that blood cells float in

racial prejudice (RAY-shuhl PREJ-uh-diss) Hatred or unfair treatment of people because of the color of their skin

red blood cells (RED BLUHD SELZ) Cells in the blood that carry oxygen from the lungs to the cells and tissues of the body

segregate (SEG-ruh-gate) To separate or keep groups of people apart

tuberculosis (tu-bur-kyuh-LOH-siss) A highly contagious disease that usually affects the lungs

Index